INTUITIVE POEMS:
A Woman's Journey

By

Lesley Clark

Dear Veronica,
  Enjoy these words of
wisdom! Life is one
experience after another to
help our soul grow

Love,
Les

INTUITIVE POEMS: A Woman's Journey

Copyright © 2008 by Lesley Clark

Dedication

Through the singing of my soul, I have created a treasure chest of my poems for the world to enjoy. I dedicate this book to anyone who has ever desired to hear their own soul. It is our natural inner voice that guides each and every one of us through the lives we have chosen. All we have to do is listen.

Acknowledgments

Thank you to Kathleen Loughery for encouraging me to trust my inner voice and to express what flows through me naturally and to Karen Rojas Henry for giving me the first blank journal and inspiring me to record all my heartfelt poems. To all my friends and family who have been patiently waiting for this book. Thank you to Allan and Bill for all their help in creating this book. Cover portrait painted by Marian P. Clark. I am truly grateful for the inspiration from my inner voice that kept me writing continuously.

Table of Contents

The Magic of Words

I have a talent which encompasses a truth
I have had it since my youth

On any level
I always will revel

My poems come forward in a rushing flow
At the end I am left with a glow

They all come out in a matter of minutes
Sometimes I do not even know what is in it

At times I will not read my rhyme
Until the next day in my own time

Many words flow through my soul
Some of the outcome I already know

A Gift Disguised

One always thinks tears
Are fears

But what if we couldn't use our tears like I cannot today
I really want to because it is what I am feeling in every
way

I feel like crying
A part of me is sad not dying

I need a release to let go
If I could cry I know

That I would feel better because all my emotion through
my tears expresses
My sadness would be laid to rest

And when I was through
I would feel enlightened no longer blue

So what I say about tears
Is they are a gift I have used through out my fifty years

In my journey on this planet
That is where my soul landed

I will never think about tears as fear
I will see them as cleansing myself is that clear

The Hard Exchange

I called the heart lobotomy institute
Requesting a heart substitute

They said come on down
This time they would make sure I received one with top
quality for my second time around

I drove one hundred miles
When I arrived I saw smiles

A team was waiting
To fix up my heart so I could start dating

It only took forty five minutes
Then I was in it

My re-programmed heart I was ready to go out and start
Being open to the handsome men with big hearts

You see I could not remember anything about how I felt
before
The old heart was gone all of it and more

Someone mentioned the name Norton, did not ring a bell
Sort of like an empty shell

I looked at someone's hands
No memory, reminded me of a clam

Lips
My knees didn't dip

Well, they were successful the surgery went well my heart
memory was gone
I am now singing all new songs

The Rhythm of Life

Time
It takes us down the line
Sometimes we feel we need to rush, we are in a hurry
Scurry, scurry, scurry

If we just learn to relax and realize time is our friend
Everything will know where to end
Time can work against or for us
When we are waiting on love we lust

Time is a divided explosion
Up and down where is the notion
Truly I believe it works in ones favor
We usually do not understand a cutting edge razor

All things happen in life when we are ready, it is true
You cannot move into a relationship if you are blue
So time comes to visit again
To show you what is now and what was then

Time is really on our side
It presents itself when there is no lie
Everything has been worked through
All of it benefits you

If the timing is not right
We will never see the light
The life experience will be gone
All wrong

So respect I have for time
There is my dime

Feelings

My eyes are golden
My heart is showing

All the love I have inside
Which I choose not to hide

Love and feelings
Send you reeling

Listening to your gut
Keeps one out of a rut

Feelings of contentment from within resonate within my
being
Can you hear me sing?

Joy love and happiness
Then a kiss

Oh what a feeling my heart feels
My lips are closed not sealed

My body relates
To this very date

How is one supposed to be?
In life happy and free

That is where I am now and where I choose to stay
Solid and strong by the way

The Healing Process

The Clark rehabilitation center in west L.A. caters to the
stubborn in each and every way
Every single day

First of all they are firm
While educating you so you can learn

About listening and having faith
Will only help you to relate

To the needs of your body, ones temple they preach
All is in ones own reach

They have strict rules for your benefit only
The staff never leaves you lonely

Attending to all of your needs
We aim to please

Part of the education that differs here
Is you need to listen and have trust, a must or they clean
out your ears

Each patient that leaves is always healed
Because they had the real deal

Which was becoming in tune by listening to their bodies,
classes included in the stay and oh by the way

We have not had a repeat patient as of yet
I guess the common sense session was met

With a sudden click
Nope none of this was a trick

What really happened was every injured person had to
teach each new patient what they learned about recovery
As it turned out the secret was patience, trust, faith, and a
little self discovery

The center is now rated number one and pretty popular
For all the patients this was never a blur

Heaven

Heaven is a place where many souls reside
We on earth use this name and cannot hide

For this is a place where we all will be
Someday you see

At least our souls know
That we have no control once we go

But the human mind
Only learns in time

So this rhyme is for those who can open up and see
There is a world beyond what we believe

No need to worry or fuss
It is not a must

For all to understand
The vast difference between the world and man

We are taught one thing
The universe has a different ring

Once one is exposed
They never know

How far they will see
The key is to accept and let it be

Unspoken

Women can relate to words
Because we always want to be heard

Feeling down to ones soul
With words they are solid and you know

No guessing games
Nothing all the same

For you have chosen to share
What you truly feel not purchased a card that is already
out there

You took the time
Maybe to create your own rhyme

If not you expressed yourself without any help it comes
down to you did it your own way, you chose the start
Extracted the words from your heart

Sharing them from within
Your own skin

That is a sign
You took the time

This means to a woman
You are of quality for certain

We all know men are wired in a different way it does not
mean they cannot bend and say
What they feel in there heart on any given day

For there does not have to be a special occasion

Love can dry up like a raisin

It is the little gestures
They are wonderful, we sure do treasure

So thanks for opening up
All the heart felt stuff

Inner Beauty

It is not about looks
One could be a crook

It is about ones heart and soul
I hope every one knows

All it takes is one precious moment to see
What that person is about let it be

Because the inner composition of ones soul
Is what you should fully know

The shell the outside
Will misguide

You
Can often make you blue

But once you get to know ones heart and soul
You will never guess you will always glow

The Waiting Dating Game

For men there may be many a match
But not one that I truly want to catch

Because I have lived and felt
The one man who made me melt

So I am out there just to find
The one who can fit into my rhyme

I am out there and free to let it be and see
Who the universe has brought me

At times I think there is no one else and I am to be alone
Only to roam

But in my heart
I truly feel there is a new start

In the relationship world
Many colors I think swirl

For now
I must learn to accept the how

It will all come together
Because the picture I hold and believe is clever

So I will not doubt
Nor will I shout

I will just trust
Enjoy any lust

Be present

Let go of all and any resentment

Because the universe knows the plan
And can

Set it into motion any time any day
When it is meant to be it will come my way

Unraveled

I peel my skin
To see within

My soul is a deep funnel
Such as a long tunnel

Turns, twists, up and down, round and round
Only the humming of a sound

Thoughts and feelings surface
But I am not nervous

Effected I am
Not by a man

But my vision of the world
Lumped together and curled

Intertwined and complicated
Two steps away I feel elated

Baring all
As if not to fall

Darting with my feelings
Until they stop reeling

Who knows what one truly has going on inside their head?
Once you feel a feeling it becomes dead

You feel it, move past it, and grow
Traveling on to the next show

Life is but one lesson after another you see

Each one has special lessons, mine are for me

We All Have Intuition

I totally lead with my heart and my gut
Right away I know where to cut

The feelings off from my mind
We know which one always shines

Getting stuck in a thought process that does not feel right
Is like a haunting at night

Everything in life has come too fast
If we do not listen to our gut it will not last

So signs we must be grateful for
Always choose not to ignore

For they are gifts to honor and be aware
So we can enjoy life without a care

Differences

Do you know what makes the world go around?
Variety you do not require a sound

If everybody was the same
The world would be lame

It is so wonderful that everyone has a different way of
thinking
How could anybody be shrinking?

Enough of every thought from every view
Each time we hear all brand new

That is why it is positive for opposites to attract
After spending time together, they learn not lack

Sharing, caring, and listening how each one believes
Helps the other to see

Communication is the key across the board
That is a must, so it can always be an open door

Freeing of One's Soul

I am finally using my intuition
To make all my decisions

I am being guided
By the light

This built in feeling resonates from my gut
Keeping me continuously out of a rut

All life answers are within me
Can't you see?

You must clear out the clutter
And open the shutters

Every thought and emotion that goes unresolved piles on
You must release all of it until it is gone

That is why one must work through all of your issues
Even if you have to use one hundred tissues

Love Described

What is love?
A feeling in your soul that warms you from up above

You look at the world from a different place
Floating along as if you were in outer space

Everything is brighter
You even feel lighter

The place in your heart that you feel
Runs through your whole body it is real

Love is a feeling of happiness, joy, and caring
Something you always want to be sharing

You give your heart and soul freely without a thought
This I hope you were taught

The feeling you felt in your body fiber
Could not take you any higher

It is euphoric, no other way to explain it
Your whole body is lit bit by bit

Within

It is important in life to discover your passion
If you are lucky, it can keep you cashing

In on what floats your survival on this planet, in this
lifetime
Keep searching it will help you shine

As you sit and listen to your inner words of wisdom
Soon enough you will come up with a decision

On which direction you choose to flow
Take a deep breath and let it all go

Quiet your mind
The answers will come back to you in time

When your mind is too busy
One feels dizzy

You may not believe, but the answers are all there
Take some time because you care

Listen to your gut and your heart
If you do, you will be off on a great start

Remember this is your life, your experiences, your journey,
and most of all your choice
If you choose to have a voice

The Formation

Where does one learn, and how do we become who we are
It starts with our parents who can take us so far

A lot of life is picked up along the way
Because we learn something new each day

Events and people flow in and out of our life which creates
an effect on us
We pick what we value add it to our being and the rest is
dust

See we are our own creators in this world every hour every
minute
As we sit in it

Everything we do is by choice
We all have a voice

It is like a mountain of sand
Form it and let it scatter all over the land

Rely on Yourself

I have learned in my life that there are meaningful things
Connected to long strings

That is where one begins and where one ends
But who does lend

Their idea to you
The old woman that lives in a shoe

Knowing it is just your imagination soaring high
Thinking you can fly

For one never really knows
How life goes

Trusting your intuition keeps you strong
Trust your intuition and you will never be wrong

Because all you need to know
Your gut will tell you so

Remember your heart and your head are different, your
mind will only tell you time
But your heart will tell you the truth all the way down the
line

Cruising Along

I am so there
Without a care

In tune with my journey on this planet earth
Riding the wild waves of the surf

Feeling each moment now
Enjoying the experience and how

Tonight I feel grounded and euphoric
Not caloric

Wrapped up in my soul, pleased with my life at the time
Because I have created a reason sharing all my rhymes

Expanding all that is within my soul
So nothing takes a toll

On my heart, body, mind, and spirit
All my choices are within it

I gaze along
Feeling oh so strong

I have created my life steering in the right direction of
growing and learning
Every which way I will be turning

My destiny will flow
Assisting me as I grow

Distinction

I learned in two thousand four that there are grey areas in
life
It is not always black and white

Even though we choose what we feel
Pushing away the real deal

Because of life's boundaries and earthly rules
If you only knew you truly did not have a clue

It is not only what one can see with the naked eye
We must learn to trust our own feelings they never lie

The intuition that comes from within
Is never dim

Bright as a light
Lighting up the night

A combination of all of our senses never leaves room for
guessing
With our life we will not be messing

As we learn to listen to our own voice
We will choose it every time as our choice

Enjoyment

It has been quite a while since I truly enjoyed myself
I no longer require help

To be set free
So I could truly see

That nothing but myself
Created what I thought I needed which was help

What I needed was to be calm and look around
Pull myself up from the ground

Because nothing was wrong
I was always strong

I just had a belief
Once I let that go guess what came along, my relief

So I want to share
Do not let life give you a scare

Because we create what we believe is real
Live in the now that is the real deal

The Way It Is

When the heart sings
And one does not carry any strings

Freedom from within happens, we let go of life and let it be
Then we can really see

How everything comes together and gels
The experiences of life tells

A story
Oh glory

Similarities

Life and dating
Both keep you waiting

So once you understand
About how life and a man

Are in a sense the same
You will not feel the need to play games

Life happens and there is no timing, we must be patient
And get to know the man before we can have a relation

When you let everything in your life flow
You become clear on what you are learning and then you
know

So take them both slow enjoy each moment do not rush to
get to the next stage
It will confuse the journey and skip a page

Each and every experience is meant to happen at its own
pace
Remember life and getting to know a man is not a race

The Flower

As one listens to their gut they become clearer
Manifesting what is near

When you treat yourself with respect
You get

So much more out of your daily life, you are true to you
You blossom and never question who

You are, you know
It begins to grow and show

In every aspect
Everyone can detect

Everyone can see
What should shine through and be

It is you unfiltered, unsung
Look at all the work you have done

The end result is peace within your soul
Try it and you will know

No game no disguise
Be grateful you are not living a lie

Trust Your Soul

Sometimes I think about our planet and all it has to offer
wonderful everything to enhance our life
We should all realize the connection the ties

To everything
All together one ring

If we all choose to look at the bright side
Not be consumed and ready to hide

When life gets tough
And each one of us has had enough

If one could focus on the reality of the beauty this earth has
to give we would all live a calm life
One would be optimistic and continue to strive

To stay on course for their own journey
Never leaving you empty and yearning

Because one's vision would be so clear
Unclouded and near

The positive healing light of your life would shine through
Giving strength to you

Your heart, your health what is important would stand out
Your soul would no longer have to shout

It would not have to fight so hard to make us understand
that we all can live our dream
Easy it is and it seems

That once we let go

29

We would all know

That our soul will guide us as it is meant to be
Because life is truly all about lessons can't you see?

Eye Opener

I am learning I am growing
One soul by itself never has all the knowing

As I dive deep
I reap

All the benefits of my searching
Open one door something is lurching

I decide to break it apart
So whatever it is does will not start

To fester and take control
This I realize and know

That coming to terms with what is can only lighten my load
It makes for a wonderful journey down the road

Because all we have is the moment
Which the mind cannot show it

Once one clears the air
Releases all the scare

You are left with peace
That is when you truly are released

From the chatter the mess
No test

Just what it was truly in front of you
Remember to focus on the now and be true to you

There Is Always a Second Chance

The first time around love was not hard
Almost like flipping a coin for a card

This time it is later in life and we have a history, I knew I
was aware
Except the circumstances are heavy and oh how I care

I am level headed and try to ground myself each day
It did not work right as it should this way

I exploded because I am over loaded with emotion
A turbulent ocean

I often wonder why
To release it I cried

Let it all go
Now I know

That one should never hang on
When it is time to go remember to let it be gone

What Is Hidden

Follow your heart, follow your heart
Right from the start

Never let go of what you truly feel
Your intuition is real

Guiding you along
Happy happy songs

All these feelings from down inside
Are not meant to hide

They are meant to be shared
With the special one that cares

The one that rocks your soul
You know

That excitement that feeling
You are reeling

Nothing can take away the deep rooted sensation
You created your own nation

Now you are at peace
Love is within your own reach

Just have a vision
It will come to fruition

Gratitude

The simple comforts and pleasures of life I will not take
lightly anymore
I hear them knocking at my door

What one can take for granted
Leaves us empty handed

Sitting in our own sorrow
Not being thankful to enjoy the comfort of tomorrow

I know I should be thankful for each day
For it has brought me peace in every way

When one does not appreciate the little things
Something happens and the upset bell rings

Be focused and live in the now
So you can see the wow

Do not dig yourself in too deep
Or you will not reap

Life's pleasures
Which are not to be measured

Always Welcome Change

The world is ever changing
Our lives re-arranging

As we go with the flow
We learn more you know

If we resist
A bunch of empty picks

For the world moves in one direction
Resistance is not a free election

Everything on the planet happens for a reason
Just like the four seasons

People cross paths and have life lessons
Experience keeps us guessing

Fresh and new ideas are formed
But we are not always forewarned

We put the idea into play
The process flow each and everyday

If we become stagnant beings
We would only hear the same bell ring

Life would be boring and dry
That is why

We must go with the flow and welcome change, open your
heart and mind
Remember it all works out in its own divine time

Individuality

Nobody is in my shoes or will ever be
Because they were designed only for me

No mixing on people's journeys
We are all separate no yearning

Exploring our own paths
Not blaming other's aftermath

Watch your life unfold
It is gold

If you choose to push away the clutter
Leaving room for another

Life lessons are far apart and in between
They all offer what should be seen

Displays of sometimes what we cannot imagine
Accept it, sometimes it is not rationed

It is set up before we come here
Choosing from the other side what we should learn be-
comes near

I know it is hard to do I have struggled myself, but let it
flow
Because the energy always knows

Life's Road

Life is much like a silk scarf
Beautiful colors roaming around in one's heart

That is not how it starts, it grows slowly
Hopefully you will not be lonely

Because you will see all that it can offer the big picture
over a period of time
Plenty of reasons keep reading this rhyme

As you grow you will learn and know
That if you let life's choices flow

It will truly show that the path you chose
Will not hose

You up in sorrow or pain
You will ultimately gain

From your life lessons
So don't be a messin

With the natural flow of life it is there for a reason
Relax and experience every season

The Gift of a Pen

Journaling takes what is circling in your head
Brings the words into reality to be read

To make one aware and see the light
Revealing true thoughts written each night

A wonderful tool soothing, comforting, and real
Instead of sharing your spiel

Your sacred words of wisdom that you expressed yourself
Without anyone's help

Opened your own eyes to see
What needed to be

What Really Matters

Love is not for sale
It can get stale

It is up to the ones involved
To solve

Any hiccups that come along
Doesn't matter who is wrong

That is not the issue at hand
It is who can

Understand
That there are differences between a woman and a man

This will go on through life
So remember men choose a wife

That lights your fire
And women make sure that man sends you higher

The sky is the limit in love
Search the stars up above

Remember to be true in your heart
From the very start

The Release

I desire a cracker and a kiss
Marital bliss

A union between two
Not all about you

Two souls come together
Expecting to leave each other never

One never knows
About one's soul

For the journey, the life, the ties
The emptiness, the cries

Life is so precious we can never predict what path we will
be on
It just comes along

Always go
With the natural flow

Follow your heart and listen to your gut
This will always keep you out of a rut

Nurture your inner being
Hear it sing

With joy and love
Sent from heaven up above

Remember there is a bigger picture always, we just cannot
see
Because we must focus on the now and let it be

Reflection

It is important to take time to reflect on each day
Do it in your own way

Choose to make the time
It doesn't have to rhyme

Take care of your emotions
So life does not run together into a huge ocean

That way you will have a handle on the choices you make
Baking your own cake

The Surprise

Whatever is coming to me
Is great you see

For twists and turns in life just happens, the key is to let it
flow
One must learn this and know

There are no road blocks or stop signs we must follow
The truth is never hollow

All those little gifts that we have been given along the way
Need to be acknowledged each day

Moving too fast and not enjoying the moments that will
last
Will only send us into the past

It will stunt our growth
Far away, remote

So being aware
Showing we care

Truly being thankful for all the signs
Answers our reason and rhyme

Who's Viewpoint

You follow your heart and your dreams
Then there are no schemes

For life is crazy
Do not get lazy

Because the world is at your finger tips
Let go of all the low dips

Focus on the way you want to live your life on this planet
Do not let it become stagnant

You are the creator of your own path
Look at life as a craft

A fun, interesting, creative journey
Please remember we are all here for the learning

Once you pass through one lesson
There will be another one and it may keep you guessin

Growing and expanding your inner being
Will make exciting bells ring

Your attitude will carry you through
So remember stand at the angle in life that gives you the
most positive view

Because this is your life and it is all about what you your-
self choose
How can you lose?

The Natural Flow

Well, what a week
I am glad I did not have a peek

Of what was to come
Life undone

We never know what is in store
Life reveals itself more and more

No need to worry or plan ahead
Ideas and life become dead

Changing all the time
A penny for your thoughts I am offering a dime

That split second thought that flashes through my mind
I am not always catching time after time

I must pay closer attention and listen to the voice
It is sending the right choice

Now I am semi hit out of left field
Learning to deal

With loss once again
Some things just never end

They go away for a while
Then come back around with a smile

The best way to live on this planet is to go with the flow
It is the truest, easiest way I know

So I will begin tomorrow

This will leave little room for sorrow

When you flow with the energy and let all of it go
Life will show you the truth that is so

Listen

My whole world turned around from one thought
Something early on I was not taught

The vision that came through tonight
Felt just right

Things in your life can stand still
Feeling as if there is not a thrill

Then they show themselves from another angle
We then become untangled

It all becomes quite clear, just as if one is being guided
from within to expand
So you can land

Straight up
With your full cup

Silence is the key
Once you have that you can magically see

Peace Within

As I lay in bed with my feet under this down comforter I
realize
the pleasure of peace
Just laying here calmly gives me a release

For silence is truly golden
Sometimes one does have a lot of knowin

Tonight my soul is calm
There is no self alarm

Pleasant treasures
This cannot be measured

Envelope my soul
This I feel and know

I can hardly explain
Why there is no more emotional pain

I am back from the journey
I left behind all the yearning

I know how to handle my words
Not fight with them because they were never absurd

They were just insight
Into a certain part of my life

The Detachment

As I learn and grow
I never thought I would know

How my life would change
And my thoughts re-arrange

As we expose ourselves
We see the new help

That life has placed before ones eyes
The experiences resonates and then we realize

The change that occurs
Is never a blur

Because you have walked through your own experience
that you have lived and felt
Not asking for help

Once one lives through anything that is true
There is not a question within you

You know
What should show

Your heart tells you so
Your gut truly does know

So I say
Be kind to yourself each and every day

Peeling Back the Layers

Life shall be what it shall be
Once you surrender it is easier you see

For there is always a bigger picture we just do not know
The stars, the earth, and the planets tell us so

For alignment in one's life is truly the turning point that
brings through
The real you

Focused, clear and clean
Honest and in tune is what I mean

Nothing gets in the way
We can see beyond the clutter each day

So remember there is more than just life's surface stuff
Dealing with all of the issues and letting them go is enough

To bring you to your place of peace
Then you will be able to release

All that is not positive in your world
Watch it as your wonderful journey becomes uncurled

The Present

The flowers the trees
The blossoms the leaves

Spring, summer, winter, fall
Look at the seasons and enjoy them all

We miss too much along the way
One never wants to be sorry about a day

The beauty on earth the colors we see
Are so natural and amazing that is key

Have you ever noticed the vibrant color in a flower?
Thank you for the rain they always need a shower

Just as the human soul needs to be nurtured, it fills us up
It is always a loving cup

Focusing on the positive in life
Is so very wise, truly nice

Then one can
Lend an understanding hand

Because they have moved ahead
Smooth words already read

A heart and a soul combined who shall know
That a flower and a soul both explicit beauty that shows

Choices

Life will always throw you a curve
It usually hits a nerve

It is all for one's own growth so one can learn and see
The bigger picture so embrace it and let it be

We all think we know
How life's road will go

But the twists and turns, stops and pops
Seem to happen a lot

Life is what you create
Sometimes we are late

In our self discovery and then we choose to change what is
already old
Deciding to transform and go for the gold

This is the greatest thing about life; it is flexible decisions
that can be changed at any time
East and west hear the chime

Once we realize that our choice shapes our future
We will begin to nurture

Our soul
This I am sure you know

The Connection

When one starts out in life they never ever know
What will take place and how it will go

So the key is to just let life happen do not try to figure out
the puzzle
Just nuzzle

Love each moment do not let one pass you by
A natural high

Release
Which will give you peace

Pray if you choose
You can never lose

Because what we all have in common on this planet is the
human connection
No we are not divided into sections

We are all one
No partitions none

Each and every one of us
Rides the same bus

The same wave
Everyday

It is only our made up rules
That causes duels

Between one another
No we should not have to hover

We should always stand tall
If one of us should start to fall

Reach out with open arms and call
To your fellow being
Now that will instantly make your heart sing

And you will see
How the relationship is between human beings

The Wonder of Life

We only have each day if we do not look ahead
Forgetting to focus on the now will leave many lines un-
read

Living in the present
Will leave no resentment

Nothing can pass us by
Because we will be alert, not shy

As we get older and gain wisdom, we become calm
Not setting off our self alarm

Priorities change
Our life preferences rearrange

Not because we planned
Accept it as a helping hand

The gift that has come
Can never be undone

Growing and learning is a part of life you see
Be grateful you are one of the ones to agree

When I think of life, I am filled with joy
Just as a child plays with a new toy

The world is yours to create
Hurry up don't hesitate

About the Author

I started writing poetry when I was seventeen while riding a city bus. That is when it all began. I have always loved words and have taken them to heart.

Expressing myself through writing has always been a way for me to transform all that is circling in my head into the physical reality. Once I achieve that, a clear picture presents itself.

In the past five years everything has changed for me and many poems flow through me on a daily basis. I believe now is the time to share what I have created.

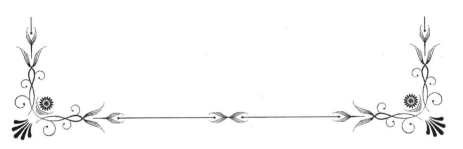

Made in the USA
Charleston, SC
21 October 2010